# GOD IS LOVE

## Hand of God Series

by

## Ernestine H. Gray, Ph.D.

*"He that loveth not knoweth not God: for God is love."*

*(I John 4:8)*

DORRANCE PUBLISHING CO., INC.
PITTSBURGH, PENNSYLVANIA 15222

The opinions expressed herein
are not necessarily those of the publisher.

ISBN # 0-8059-3938-5
Printed in the United States of America

*First Printing*

For more information or to order additional books, please write:
Dorrance Publishing Co., Inc.
643 Smithfield Street
Pittsburgh, Pennsylvania 15222
U.S.A.

# TABLE OF CONTENTS

## ACKNOWLEDGMENTS

I want to thank the many teachers, friends, pastors, family and the Holy Spirit, who have added to my life. God is continuing to perfect me even as I write this vision of His love.

A special thanks and gratitude to: my parents, Roosevelt and Claudine Herbin, who reared their four children with Godly principles; all of the adults who were a part of my youth from the many church denominations were instrumental in my growth and development in the church; and, Lois Bowen for her help with the selection of illustrations used throughout my book. I would also like to express my appreciation to those who made it possible for me to travel in conjunction with church conferences that helped to develop me as a young child in Christ.

My work experiences over the many years include, missionary trips abroad, which were supported by two past presidents of Bennett College in Greensboro, North Carolina; Dr. David D. Jones and Dr. Willa B. Player.

# INTRODUCTION

For sometime, I have had thoughts concerning the little cards we were given in Sunday School when I was a child. These cards were written very simply and a teacher could be creative in using them as lessons. Later, I noticed that Bible verses were stored in my memory and when I needed them, they kept me focused.

Through years of teaching and counseling, I have gained knowledge of how students learn even though I am still being perfected. These observations have taught me that students learn in different ways and have different needs. Therefore, these short lessons are designed to help students organize their mind, while at the same time, grow in the knowledge of the love of God. Older students or senior citizens will find these lessons equally beneficial in life. Please read the indicated Bible lessons before doing the reflection. The material may be used in many ways, a sheet may be given to students as they enter the class. Students can work independently or use it as an assignment. The reflections may be discussed. It is likely that the students' spiritual needs will surface during some of these lessons.

This book is called a *Hand of God Series* because God gave me a dream. In the dream, I saw the hand of God. In the palm of His hand were the words, "Lo, I am with you always." He instructed me to go. I knew this was a card. He told me to sign the card with the words "The Lord." I used the card to call our first family reunion. We were richly blessed.

This book is the second in the *Hand of God Series*. May God richly bless you as you continue to seek Him and make Him first in your life.

**BELIEVING**

---

## WHO ARE YOU?

---

John 1:19-26

It would be a long story to try to tell you who I am. Lord, what is this all about? I asked.

Surely, he seems to say, "You know your call. It is to write, and sound an alarm."

"It is to alert my people that there is a need for each one to hear the call...to hear my voice...to obey my voice."

"I call you by name. I call you my own."

Reflection:     Take time to pray and to seek God concerning
                who you are.

# GOD LOVES THE SON

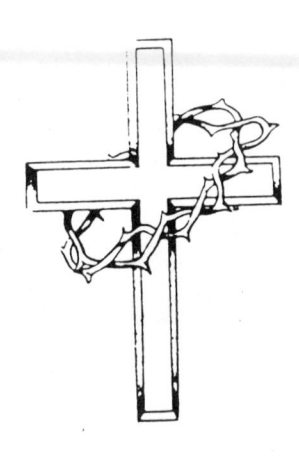

John 3:31-36

The father, who is a spirit, left his throne in heaven to come to earth in the form of a man. This was necessary in order for him to identify with man. As a man, he, also, presented himself as the son of God. As the son of God, he knew and understood the father. When he had completed his mission on earth (his death was an act of love for you and me) he went back to the father, who had given him power over all things. The son sent the Holy Spirit to abide in us and to comfort us.


Reflection:     What is my understanding of the Godhead?

# HAPPY ARE THOSE WHO TRUST IN GOD

Psalm 2:2-12

Why trust in God?  Can God do anything that the policeman, a parent, or a teacher cannot do?  Can we do everything for ourselves?  If we put all of our trust in the policeman, he may not get to the scene on time.  As hard as he tries, he may get lost.  If we think that our parents can save us, they can only believe God for us.  God has to do the saving.  If we think that we are going to get all of our wisdom from teachers, then the teachers get their wisdom from God.  We trust all these people to do their job; we must be connected to God for ourselves.

Reflection:    Memorize verse 12

# THE THINGS THAT I TEACH
# COME FROM THE FATHER

John 7:14-18

Many people did not believe Jesus. He told them that he only spoke what the Father told him to say. The people did not want to obey the Father, therefore they did not know the truth when they heard it. It would have brought honor to the father if they had wanted to obey him.

Reflection:

Some people today want to bring honor to themselves instead of bringing honor to God. They may fail to speak the truth because they do not hear God.

Think about different ways you can hear God's voice; for example, through the Bible, through the pastor, through your parents, in your own spirit, God will always speak what is in the Holy Bible. Write a paragraph about a time you heard God's voice.

# THE WORLD DOES NOT
# LIKE THE TRUTH

I Kings 22:7-8

The Lord spoke through prophets in the Old Testament. The prophets heard God's voice and gave the proper direction. There are prophets in the church today. Sometimes the pastor gives us a prophetic word.

Again, some people do not want to hear the prophet because they want to please themselves, rather than change and do what God wants.

Reflection:

Would you rather obey God, even if the people hate you, or would you rather please the people (have the people like you) and disobey God?

Which do you choose? Write why you made your choice.

# WHO IS THIS MAN

John 7:40-43

People did not know who Jesus was. Some thought he was a prophet, others thought he was the Christ. Some people wanted to arrest him, but no one could touch Jesus. Some people still do not know Jesus. The Bible says that many will come saying they are the Christ.

Reflection:

Pray that you will know the real Jesus...that He will give you discernment.

## SCRIPTURE IS ALWAYS TRUE

John 10:34 and 38                                    Psalm 82:6
John 11:25-27

Jesus referred to himself as the Son of God.

The ancestors had called their rulers "gods."

God is the Most High God; men have God given capacities
being made in his image.  Therefore, men live forever (see
Revelations 6:9).

Reflection:

When you really understand what is meant by a passage, the
passage often becomes more believable.  Tell how you grew in
your understanding and belief today.

# THE PLAN TO KILL JESUS

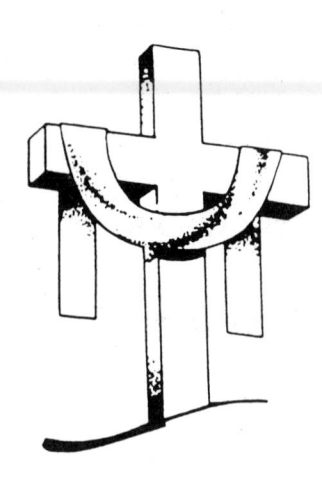

John 11:45-57                                    Luke 9:23 - 25

The High Priest (not a follower of Jesus) prophesied that Jesus
would die for the Nation as well as those children scattered
abroad.  Even though the High Priest had said so,
some people were troubled with unbelief.  Despite the evidence,
they refused to see the glory of God.  The decision was made to
reject Jesus and do away with him.

The leaders feared losing their esteem.

Reflection:

Is there anything in your life that you are holding on to rather
than to deny yourself and meet the needs of people?  Are you
rejecting Jesus in any way?  Write out your conclusion/your
decision.

# THE LORD IS KING FOREVER AND EVER!

Psalm 10:1-18

Sometimes we may feel that the enemy has advanced when we see the wickedness in our society. Sometimes, we may say "Where is God?"

If we know that God sees and knows all things, then we know that nothing is hidden from him. We have to trust God for justice to be done.

Reflection:

Pray that our leaders, religious as well as secular will be surrounded by Godly council.

Have you received persecution in your life? If so, meditate on Psalm 10:16-18.

## HEALING

---

### DO YOU WANT TO BE MADE WELL?

---

John 5:1-8

In this world, it seems that many people are sick in some kind of way. There are many needs all around us. The man at the pool had no one to help him. He had no family or friends to help. We see that Jesus has the power to meet the needs of every person in this world.

Reflection:

Meditate on verses 6-8

# WHY WE WERE CREATED?

Isaiah 43:1, 7, 21

God created us for his glory.  We show forth his glory by
praising him and by being obedient to his voice.  It is He who
has created us and saved us.  We belong to him.  We
are his handiwork.

Reflection:

Since God created you, he knows how to repair any parts of
your being that need repair.  Examine yourself.  Is there
anything about yourself that needs changing?  Write the things
down that you feel need changing.  Discuss with a Christian,
counselor, teacher, or parent so you can pray, praise and
commit it to God.

# GOD HAS POWER OVER
# SICKNESS AND DISEASE

II Kings 4:32-33

The prophet prayed before he rendered "resuscitation" as we might call it today. Perhaps, he got his direction from God concerning what he should do for this child's healing. God can cause healing many different ways.

Reflection:

Look up the following scriptures and tell how healing took place. Isaiah 38:32, Proverbs 4:20 - 22, Proverbs 17:22. Find another healing scripture on your own.

# WHAT DO YOU SAY ABOUT HIM?

John 9:13-34

There was a man who healed a man on the Sabbath. The
Pharisees said that Jesus was not from God because he healed
on the Sabbath. They could not agree with each other. The man
had to answer the question concerning who Jesus was for
himself. His parents could not answer for him. He had to
admit that he was a follower.

Reflection:

Do you think the man was afraid? How did he tell the
Pharisees that Jesus healed him? How was this man a good
teacher? Have you ever been ashamed/afraid to tell what Jesus
did for you? How did you overcome?

## GOD HAS GIVEN US POWER OVER SICKNESS AND DISEASE

John 12:27-36

Jesus knew that his death was near. He felt the agony, not because he feared death, but because his nature was holy and his death was associated with sin. Jesus had no sin. His death on the cross was a sacrifice for our sins. The message of the Church is - the CROSS which draws all men.

Reflection:

Jesus took glory in suffering and dying. Can you sing a song of "thanksgiving"? If not, keep trying!

Release your problems, whether sin, sickness or disease, to God.

## PROTECTION

---

## I AM THE GOOD SHEPHERD

---

John 10:1-21

The Good Shepherd (Jesus) knows his sheep. He calls them by name. He leads them. Jesus is the door for the sheep. (We are the sheep) The good shepherd gives his life for the sheep. The sheep listen to his voice; the sheep know the shepherd.

Reflection:

As you read the lesson you not only saw what the Good Shepherd does. You saw some of the ways that sheep act ... tell some of these ways.

How has Jesus been a good Shepherd to you?

## THE LORD IS MY SHEPHERD

Psalm 23; John 10:11

Jesus is the good shepherd who gave his life for the sheep. He leads the sheep in paths of righteousness everyday. We can place all of our cares and needs in his hands. We do not have to fear. He gives us comfort. We can trust him.

Reflection:

Praise God today for the many ways that He is with you. Record some of these ways so that you can remember to share them.

## PROVISIONS

---

### THE LIGHT SHINETH IN DARKNESS: AND THE DARKNESS COMPREHENDED IT NOT

---

John 1:1-5

I look around and I can see the light of the S U N shining bright upon this pad as I write. I look within and I know that the light of the S O N (His light) is shining within me.

Even though there is a breeze, there is warmth from the sun. The sun is so bright,it gives light to the skies. It comes through the clouds. I think this is God's provision for me this day...light, beauty, love, joy; Yes, God is love to me.

Reflection:

Write your own thoughts about how God's light shines in your world.

# WHERE IS MY MOTHER?

John 2:1-5

Has she gone?  Is she here?  Will she come?  Will she respond?
I need my mother.  She knows the answer.  She can talk to
those who cause me trouble.  Where is my mother?

Please mother, hear my plea.  I need you now, more than ever.
Where is my mother?  My mother is in heaven, I heard the
spirit say.  She did her job.  She trained me well.  Now, I say
to you, hear the call.  Someone's mother is crying out for you.

Reflection:

Tell how you have felt a mother's love.

# THE LOVE OF GOD REACHES
## WHEREVER YOU ARE

Psalm 36:1-9

Jesus came from heaven to die on earth. He conquered the devil while on earth. He descended into hell and took Satan's keys. He returned to heaven where he is praying to the father for you and me. The father gave him all power. He can reach us no matter where we are. He hears us before we call.

Reflection:

Write out a prayer that God answered for you that showed his goodness toward you.

## LET US REJOICE AND BE GLAD

Psalm 118:24-29

I am so happy. I can run down the path. I can smell the flowers blooming. I can see the rose. I can hear the birds. I can feel the breeze. I can walk among the trees. I can swing very high. I know He loves me. I am happy.

Reflection:

Tell what makes you happy.

# I PRAISE YOU, LORD

Isaiah 12                                    II Chronicles 20:21

I praise you, Lord, for my salvation.
I praise you, Lord, because I can shout and I can sing.
I praise you, Lord, because of your greatness.
Every day of my life, I Find new ways to praise you.
I find new things for which to praise you.

Reflection:

Name 15 things for which you give the Lord praise today.
Then, stand up and give him the praise.

# HOW DO YOU HONOR GOD?

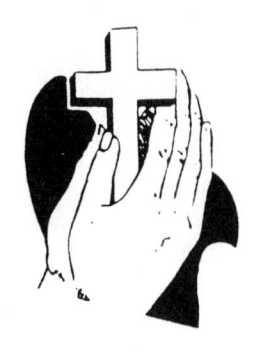

John 8:42-55

When a person introduces a speaker to the audience, they must know something about the person. They must know something that would cause the audience to want to hear the speaker. The person knows what the speaker does and something about his life. This honors the person when he is introduced correctly.

Jesus knew the Father and the Father honored Jesus. Jesus obeyed the Father, and showed his love for us when he died on the cross for us.

Reflection:

How do you honor God in your daily life? Write a paragraph introducing Jesus as the speaker.

# LORD, I HONOR YOU AND PRAISE YOU

Isaiah 25:1, 89

God's righteous people can sing praises throughout history, at the final judgement all people will honor God and praise him for his wondrous acts. Those unrighteous people will remember they did not praise him.

Lord, we praise you because you are good and your mercy endures forever. We praise you because you are the great creator and you are worthy to be praised. We praise you because you delivered us from darkness into your marvelous light.

Reflection:

Continue with praise throughout the day.

**SALVATION AND MIRACLES**

---

WE WILL LIVE WITH THE LORD

---

Psalm 101:6-8

The Lord went to prepare a place for those who love him. That means that we will see him and live with him. There will be no more lying, no more cheating, no more stealing, and no more killing, no more sin.

There will be peace. Where God is there is love, because God is love.

Reflection:

What am I doing to be ready for the Lord when he returns?

# HE TOLD ME EVERYTHING I EVER DID

John 4:39-42

Why do you believe the Bible?  Is it because you know God?
Is it because you know his character?

I can believe a trusted friend, because the friend always tells me
the truth.  The Samaritan woman knew Jesus was telling her the
truth.  When we face God at the judgement, there will be a
record of our deeds.

If we have sins in our life and confess our sins to him, and ask
him to forgive us, he is quick to forgive us all of our sins and
they will never be remembered again.

Reflection:

For your personal benefit, ask God if there is anything you need
to repent of.  Example: Do you need to forgive someone.  If
necessary, get a pastor, teacher, or parent to help you.

# THE LORD'S SUPPER

John 6:53-58

It is important to understand what it means to eat the flesh of Jesus and to drink his blood. When we have communion (The Lord's Supper) we are identifying (believing) with the death of Jesus. We are remembering that he shed his blood that we may have eternal life. It means we are joined to God. We feed on Him through faith and take on His divine nature.

Reflection:

What does eternal life mean to you?
What price did Jesus pay for your salvation?

# YOU CAN DO IT

Numbers 13:25-30

We are faced with choices every day. There are forces that will tell you that you cannot make it. These forces would cause you to lose faith. In order to succeed and do well you must have faith in God's word. If you do not have faith, you will see giants, rather than a strong God.

Caleb said, "We are able to overcome."

Reflection:

List some difficult situations that make you feel like you cannot make it. Use your faith to be like Caleb and make your declaration of being able to overcome through Jesus Christ.

# THE PRICE OF SIN

Isaiah 64:5-7

God does not like sin. God cannot look at sin. He sent Jesus, who had no sin, into the world to die and shed His blood to redeem us from our sins.

If we do not accept Jesus as Lord and Savior, there is a big price to pay. We are destroyed. Jesus has already paid the price for our salvation.


Reflection:

Describe what the Bible says it is like to be dirty with sin. (Isaiah 64:5-7)

# I AM THE LIGHT

John 8:12-20; 30-37

If you were going on a long journey, would you rather be able to see your way? Would you rather have a map or would you rather grope around in the dark.

If you said that you would rather be able to see (know) your way, then Jesus is the light. Jesus is the way. He said that he was the light. He was his own witness and the Father was another witness to the fact that he was the light. You can have that light deep down in your soul. The eyes are like a mirror of that light.

Jesus said if you continue to obey my teaching, you are my followers. You will know the truth and the truth will set you free.

Reflection:    Write out a truth in this Bible lesson that you
               wish to remember.

# DO YOU KNOW GOD LOVES YOU?

John 3:6 - 18                    Romans 3:23; 6:23

When we believe in Jesus Christ, we will have everlasting life. We will live with God forever. There will be peace and joy.

God loved us so much he gave his only begotten Son to die for us. If we do not receive the gift of God, we have eternal death.

Reflection:

Write out John 3:16-18 on a card. Write out Romans 3:23 and 6:23.

Memorize and use these verses to witness to someone.

# THE PLOT TO KILL LAZARUS

John 12:9-13

Many people had come to Jerusalem for the Passover and heard that Jesus had raised Lazarus from the dead. They were convinced that Jesus was the Messiah. They were happy and shouting praises. Wherever Jesus was, there was action and people gathered around.

Later, some people wanted to destroy Lazarus in order to prove Jesus could not raise him from the dead.

Reflection:

My prayer today is that you will smell the sweet aroma of the Rose of Sharon. Don't be surprised if those who do not believe, do not understand you.

## GOD IS LOVE

If you want your students to grow in the knowledge, grace and love of God, it will happen as they consistently work through the lessons presented in this booklet.

Each student can have his personal copy of the booklet. He can go back and review it periodically. As the student reads and reflects, he will gain a deeper level of spiritual maturity and God's love will begin to be reflected in the life of the student.

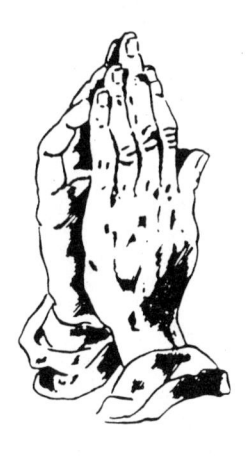

## PRAYER

Father, I thank you that the Lord Jesus Christ shed his blood, died and rose again for me. I confess that I am a sinner. I ask you to forgive my sins, and come into my life. Thank you for eternal life.

Be sure to continue to study the Word of God.

**EVALUATION SHEETS**

GOD IS LOVE

EVALUATION

Date _____

Student _____

As a participant in the lessons entitled "God Is Love" your feedback is important. You can help assure that the lessons are having the desired effect of helping you to become more organized, more focused for work while gaining an appreciation for the love of God.

On a scale of 1-10 (10 being the most favorable) please rank the following categories.

1.    The lessons helped me to gain an appreciation of the love of God.

Rank _____

2.    I have become more organized and prepared for my classes.

Rank _____

3.    In what way did friends, teachers, parents affect your becoming more organized/focused.

# GOD IS LOVE

## EVALUATION

**Date** _____

**Instructor** _____

As a participant in the lessons entitled "God Is Love", your feedback is important. You can help assure that the lessons are having the desired effect of helping your students become more organized, more focused for work while gaining an appreciation for the love of God.

On a scale of 1-10 (10 being the most favorable), please rank the following categories.

1.  Effectiveness of materials.

    Rank _____

2.  The lessons helped the students in gaining an appreciation for the love of God.

    Rank _____

3.  The students showed growth in being more organized and focused.

    Rank _____

## PROPHECY AND EVALUATION
## STATEMENTS

### A PROPHECY AND SOME EVALUATION
### STATEMENTS

A few years ago, a prophecy was given to Ernestine which indicated that many waters could not quench the fire of love in her bosom, and why should she just keep the fire in her bosom. The prophecy continued that if she let it out, He would come back again and again, and that it would start a barn fire. She was to open up and let others see. There are many weary people that need encouragement. Ernestine was to take off the cover as there was much good reading in the pages of her heart. They are precious pure pages that need to be shared.

Prophecy was given to Ernestine at church in Virginia.

Some responses to *God Is Love* include:

.       Good for family meditation. -- A high school teacher in Maryland

.       My mother and I have become closer since I studied *God Is Love*. -- A daughter in Corona, New York

35

- It put me in touch with aspects of my life that I need to be in touch with to be satisfied and feel comfortable. The format is "cool." -- A mother in Corona, New York

- Lessons are excellent. I believe that they will motivate the young and old as well to express themselves both orally and in writing. -- An Elder in Newark, New Jersey

- Each message was great and well put together. I enjoyed the book very much. -- A librarian in Rockville, Maryland

- I will recommend that our ladies consider you as their Women's Day speaker. -- A pastor in Washington, D.C.

- Consider doing a workshop for us. -- A pastor in Oxon Hill, Maryland

- If you are looking for a book to teach your adolescent or teenager how to start a quiet time with the LORD, I would suggest getting *God Is Love* by Dr. Gray. -- A homemaker and former business woman in Ft. Washington, Maryland